TOWER HAMLETS

D1081533

A gaming timeline

6000 BC

First known dice are rolled. Game on!

AD 550

Chess is invented in India, and is brought to Europe 200 years later by Arabs.

1700s

Whist and solitaire become popular card games in Europe.

c. 3000 BC

Senet is first played in ancient Egypt.

800

The first playing cards are made from paper, wood and bone.

1800

The first commercial board game is produced.

1200s

The game of snakes and ladders appears in India.

1931

Lexico is invented. (It eventually becomes Scrabble.)

1981

For the first time a video game character is able to jump.

2000s

Mobile-device games become popular.

1913

The first crossword puzzle is published in the *New York World* newspaper.

1989

The first handheld electronic games hit the shops.

1972

The world's first video game console is manufactured. The first high score is achieved!

2016

Location-based AR games take the world by storm.

Game origins

Dice (Iran)

Cards and dominoes (China)

Chess (India)

Senet (ancient Egypt)

Hopscotch (ancient Rome)

Author:

Jim Pipe studied ancient and modern history at Oxford University and spent ten years in publishing before becoming a full-time writer. He has written numerous nonfiction books for children, many on historical subjects. He lives in Dublin, Ireland, with his wife and sons.

Artist:

David Antram was born in Brighton, England, in 1958. He studied at Eastbourne College of Art and then worked in advertising for 15 years before becoming a full-time artist. He has illustrated many children's nonfiction books.

Series creator:

David Salariya was born in Dundee, Scotland. He has illustrated a wide range of books and has created and designed many new series for publishers in the UK and overseas. David established The Salariya Book Company in 1989. He lives in Brighton, England, with his wife, illustrator Shirley Willis, and their son, Jonathan.

Editor: **Jonathan Ingoldby**

Editorial Assistant: **Mark Williams**

PAPER FROM
SUSTAINABLE
FORESTS

Published in Great Britain in MMXIX by
Book House, an imprint of
The Salariya Book Company Ltd
25 Marlborough Place, Brighton BN1 1UB
www.salariya.com

ISBN: 978-1-912537-07-5

SALARIYA
SCRIBO BOOK HOUSE SCRIBBLERS

© The Salariya Book Company Ltd MMXIX
All rights reserved. No part of this publication may be reproduced, stored in or introduced into a retrieval system or transmitted in any form, or by any means (electronic, mechanical, photocopying, recording or otherwise) without the written permission of the publisher. Any person who does any unauthorised act in relation to this publication may be liable to criminal prosecution and civil claims for damages.

1 3 5 7 9 8 6 4 2

A CIP catalogue record for this book is available from the British Library.
Printed and bound in China.

This book is sold subject to the conditions that it shall not, by way of trade or otherwise, be lent, resold, hired out, or otherwise circulated without the publisher's prior consent in any form or binding or cover other than that in which it is published and without similar condition being imposed on the subsequent purchaser.

Visit
www.salariya.com
for our online catalogue and
free fun stuff.

You Wouldn't Want to Live Without™

Gaming!

Written by
Jim Pipe

Illustrated by
David Antram

Series created by
David Salariya

BOOK HOUSE
a SALARIYA *imprint*

Contents

Introduction

Humans have always loved to play games, from dice games in ancient Iran over 5,000 years ago, to chess and cards in the Middle Ages. Board games were all the rage in the 19th century, and the first video games appeared over 50 years ago. Today, millions of players compete in 'massively multiplayer online role-playing games' (MMORPGs), many spending long hours battling with friends online. There are endless ways to play, from mobile apps to virtual-reality headsets, from the moment we wake up to last thing at night. And in a world of likes, shares and followers, our whole lives can feel like a game. Now try to imagine a world without games, mods or player rankings. Is it your worst nightmare?

What makes a game?

Play is one of the oldest forms of interaction – it's part of what makes us human. Pretty much anything can be turned into a game: just think of all the different sports using just a stick and a ball. In ancient times, popular games also included dice and board games. These games reflect the world in which they were created. Chess pieces with their knights and castles say a lot about life in the Middle Ages. Games about property mirror the growth of cities, and Space Invaders reflects the Space Age. In all games, elements such as rules, luck or skill combine to make them fun – and often educational as well.

RULES. Like chess, Go has a simple set of rules and pieces that can lead to incredibly complex strategies. Over 4,000 years ago, Chinese warlords used it to practise battle tactics.

Boom! Collect 200 beads and move directly to your cave!

LUCK. Whether rolling dice or picking a card, chance is an essential part of many games. Some 5,000 years ago, the first dice were cube-shaped sheep's ankle bones used by religious shamans to tell the future.

In the world of games, assets come in many forms, from lives to money. Use them up too quickly, and you probably won't last long. But keep them too long, and you could miss your chance to win!

NOUGHTS AND CROSSES was played by ancient Egyptians. Some 5,000 years later, it became one of the first video games, called OXO.

TERRITORY. Many games have squares that must be attacked or defended, like senet, shown here, a game from ancient Egypt. This game was a matter of life and death: its 30 squares represented the journey of your spirit after death.

SKILLS. Game strategy is all about planning ahead, but some tricksters will resort to anything to gain the upper hand. Spanish priest Ruy Lopez advised chess players in the 1500s to 'sit your opponent with the sun in his eyes'.

11

Just can't stop?

Do you ever get bored of games? Puppies never do! It's how they learn about the world. Lion cubs playing rough and tumble is the same, and it's no different for humans. Games have always been an important way to learn skills or how to behave, whether playing hide-and-seek to train for hunting, using plastic bricks to design amazing machines or using game money to learn about buying and selling. Your brain gets a rush of excitement when you learn a new skill or reach a new level. That's why it's sometimes difficult to stop playing.

Hide-and-seek was first described by an ancient Greek writer 2,000 years ago, but probably dates back to early humans grunting, 'Ready or not, here I come!' to their hidden friends.

Top tip

Indoor games such as bowling or ping-pong are a fun way to exercise. But be careful not to break anything. Henry VIII is said to have bowled with cannonballs. Don't try this at home!

PING-PONG. Good games never die. Ping-pong (table tennis) was first played after Victorian dinner parties, using a book to hit a golf ball over a stack of other books. In 1975, an electronic home version of the game, called Pong, became a huge hit.

UPS AND DOWNS. Snakes and ladders is based on an ancient Indian game that charts your journey through life. Good deeds take you up a ladder to nirvana, or heaven. Bad deeds result in snakes dragging you down again!

GAME OF LIFE. In the 1800s, board games often taught a moral lesson. In the Checkered Game of Life, hard work led to success, and gambling led to ruin. In 1959, this game was updated to be about getting rich and being happy.

FIGHT SCHOOL. The US Army encourages soldiers to play video games. In addition to being a way to relax, games teach military tactics while troops are away from the front line.

Players vs machines

Until computer games first appeared in the 1950s, games had to be played with real people like your mum and dad or, even worse, your annoying little brother. Back in the 1700s, mechanical marvels known as automata were created to get around this problem (though most cheated by hiding a person inside to do the thinking). Early computer games ran on giant computers that filled an entire room. By 1972, the first console games had appeared, and since then there's been one cool gadget after another, with the arrival of PC games, handheld devices, online gaming and virtual reality. Today you can play some games just by thinking!

That's some very fuzzy logic!

SCREEN TIME. In the 1940s, the first electronic game had the catchy name of 'cathode ray tube amusement device'. Early games were programmed by students and military researchers, and were displayed on small black-and-white screens. Some had no graphics at all.

AUTO-TEXT. The 'Three Automatons' were built in the 1770s by Swiss watchmaker Pierre Jaquet-Droz and his son, Henri-Louis, using thousands of tiny gears and cogs. The 'writer' could be programmed to write a message up to 40 letters long – the original tweet!

The three automatons

The writer

The artist

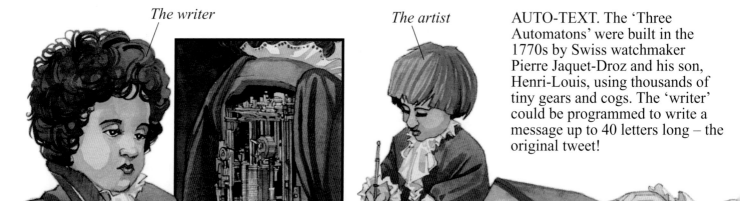

CUSTOM CONTROLLERS. In the mid-1980s, many arcade games had their own unique controllers. Racing and flying games were equipped with steering wheels and joysticks, and dancing games had pressure pads that lit up.

The musician

How it works

The first graphics were made of rows of lines, called vector images. By the 1980s, Japanese game developers had made more complex characters using 'bitmap' images created by a grid of millions of tiny dots, called pixels.

S$

MONSTER MACHINES. In the 1990s, giant arcade games appeared that were more like theme park rides, with rideable racehorses or battle pods that allowed eight players to fight in giant virtual 'mechs'.

WHAT'S THE SCORE? The world's first console, the Odyssey, was launched in 1972. Its graphics were so basic, players had to tape plastic overlays onto a TV screen as a 'board'. You also had to keep score yourself – because the machine couldn't!

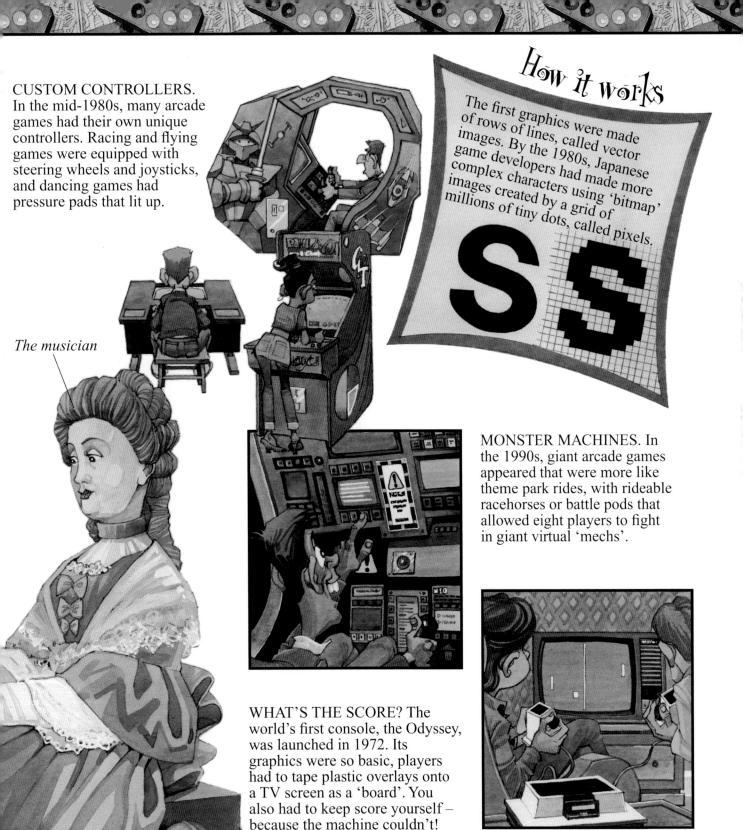

Epic wins, bad losers

Have you ever been on a long journey without any games to keep you busy? Playing games isn't just a great way to pass the time. There's the thrill of competing against others, being part of a team, the chance to get creative and the joy of an epic win after days of working through levels. Games also teach us how to overcome challenges. If you hate losing, you're in good company. Chess grandmaster Bobby Fischer called chess 'war over the board'. He wasn't joking: the son of the French king, Pepin the Short, killed an opponent by bashing him with a chess piece.

HISTORY IS FULL of bad losers. As a young man, William the Conqueror hit a French prince with a chessboard after he was checkmated.

There's only one conqueror around here!

TAKING RISKS. When playing games, half the fun is taking risks without the danger of doing it for real. Board games allow us to conquer the world, control vast sums of money, hunt down murderers or even perform a delicate operation.

I want to be banker!

You can do it!

The Roman Emperor Claudius had a backgammon board built into his chariot to keep him entertained on journeys across his giant empire. Make a list of the games you play on a long journey.

None shall game for money, either with dice or cards.

A BAD BET. Money and games don't go well together. Gambling on cards and dice often led to fights among pirates, so pirate captain Bartholomew Roberts banned it in his 'pirate code'.

TRAVEL BUG. Games are perfect for a long journey or a rainy day. Though it didn't rain much in ancient Egypt, King Tutankhamen was an avid senet player. Four different boards were found in his tomb, including a small 'travel' version.

In the zone

FANTASY FUN. The fantasy board games of the 1970s – packed with dragons, elves and wizards – were the inspiration for today's role-playing video games. These often have complex stories that take several days to play through.

When you're in the middle of a game, does time seem to stand still? Concentrating hard allows us to forget our everyday worries, whether skipping stones across a lake, building teetering towers out of wooden blocks or filling out a crossword puzzle on the train. In video games, you can go a step further, by entering a fantasy world filled with bizarre challenges and fantastical creatures. You can create your own avatar and follow your own path through a story, all while chatting with friends and family on the other side of the world.

TIED UP IN KNOTS. When Twister first appeared in the 1960s, shops wouldn't sell it – they said it was too dangerous! They changed their mind after movie star Eva Gabor played it on TV. Now it's a family favourite.

Red circle, left foot and no tickling!

GOOD GUYS AND BAD GUYS. Young children love to play games where they can take turns to be a hero or an evil villain. Many major video games (known as 'AAA' games) also allow you to choose sides, such as cops or robbers.

How it works

Successful fantasy games feel like a real place with real rules. These can get very complicated, from what happens when you jump off a waterfall to stealing loot or swallowing the wrong potion!

CAN'T STOP. Perhaps the most famous player who couldn't stop is the 18th-century Earl of Sandwich, John Montagu. He dreamed up a sliced bread snack so he could play cards all night without having to stop for a meal.

DO YOU enjoy getting into 'the zone' where you forget the world around you? It's sometimes difficult to know when to stop playing! That's what *flow* is. It happens when a game has interesting challenges that keep you focused.

Sandwich, old boy... it'll never catch on!

Brain games!

Are you a puzzle addict? There are so many to choose from: mazes, jigsaws, word searches, crosswords and online tile matching and mathematical puzzle games. Puzzles are the most popular games of all, because they can be played on so many different devices (and with pen and paper). They appeal to people of all ages, and many have a very long history. They're also perfect for learning thinking and reasoning skills, and some games may even make you smarter.

MAZES ARE among the oldest puzzles. In Greek legend, Theseus had to escape from the Labyrinth after killing the terrifying bull-headed Minotaur.

SHAPE-SHIFTING. Shapes have always fascinated us. The ancient Chinese tangram has seven shapes that can form people or animals. In 1993, Tetris – a game where shapes fit into one another – was played by Russian cosmonaut Aleksandr Serebrov aboard the MIR Space Station.

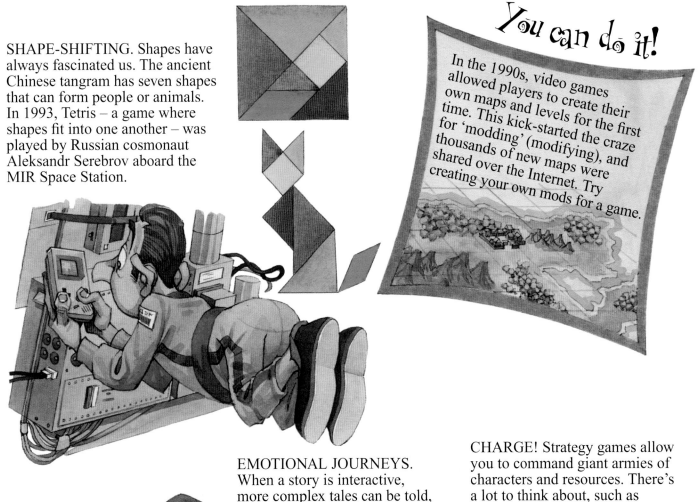

You can do it!

In the 1990s, video games allowed players to create their own maps and levels for the first time. This kick-started the craze for 'modding' (modifying), and thousands of new maps were shared over the Internet. Try creating your own mods for a game.

EMOTIONAL JOURNEYS. When a story is interactive, more complex tales can be told, allowing players to choose different paths at critical points in the game. Some video games also have incredibly moving and emotional storylines.

Sob...

CHARGE! Strategy games allow you to command giant armies of characters and resources. There's a lot to think about, such as juggling resources like food and materials, or planning a battle-winning move.

Join the clan

Gaming can be very social – whether you're making friends, chatting, working in a team or role-playing. In many games, you can only progress if you collaborate with other players. There's no shortage of people to play with: kids, teenagers, mums, dads and grandparents all play games as part of their everyday life – and at all times of the day. For some, it's a quiet game of smartphone solitaire on the bus. For others, it's screaming and shouting with a group of friends playing a racing game. The secret to having fun is knowing when to stop. There can be a lot of pressure to keep playing or keep up with other players.

TEAMWORK. There's nothing quite like a game with family or friends. If you're playing with a partner, it helps to know how they think so you can follow the same strategy!

Meet the players

Toddlers play their first games on tablets that are perfect for little fingers.

Some tween gamers take handheld gaming devices everywhere they go, sneaking in short puzzles, races and mini-games as often as they can!

Did you know that the average age of gamers is 35? Many have been playing games all their lives, switching from one device to another, as new technology and games emerge.

MASTER GAMERS. You can learn a lot about gaming from watching videos by experienced players. By 2018, one 82-year-old woman had produced hundreds of videos for her channel, describing herself as 'a grandmother who loves to play games'.

How it works

According to gaming guru Richard Bartle, every player is a mix of these four types:

- 'Killers' like to cause drama and beat other players online.
- 'Achievers' enjoy completing every level and challenge perfectly.
- 'Explorers' like to know every shortcut, trick and glitch!
- 'Socialisers' enjoy chatting and connecting with other players.

Which type describes you?

Teenage music fans can use a smartphone anywhere, anytime, to learn the hottest songs and dance moves.

About half of all gamers are women. Favourite games include social and casual games such as puzzles and farm simulations.

How long do you have?

Pressed for time? Games can take as much or as little time as you like. Sometimes you can't beat a quick game of hangman with just pen and paper, or a simple guessing game like 'animal, vegetable, mineral'. 'Speedruns' are popular with online gamers, especially on platform games. The aim is to make the game's end credits roll in just a few minutes. Other games take hours, or even days, to finish, such as a giant jigsaw puzzle or an epic role-playing saga. Serious gamers love nothing more than finishing a game after working through dozens of levels. Some strategy games can take over 600 hours to complete!

SPELL OR DIE. The grisly word game hangman dates back to Victorian times, when executions were a public spectacle. One person picks the word and the others try to guess the letters. With each wrong guess, a new piece of the 'hangman' picture is drawn.

TIME KILLER. In 1989, a game of chess played in Belgrade lasted for 269 moves. It took 20 hours and 15 minutes to complete – the longest ever in a tournament. The result? A draw!

CASUAL GAMERS. The arrival of smartphones in 2007 brought a revolution in gaming. More and more people played games when they had a few spare minutes. Casual games usually have simple rules so they can be learned quickly.

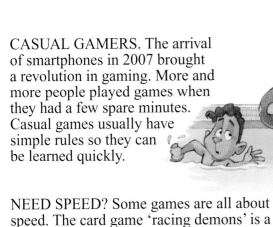

NEED SPEED? Some games are all about speed. The card game 'racing demons' is a real test of concentration and coordination, encouraging players to break all the rules by NOT waiting for their opponent to take a turn.

How it works

Speedrunners often use 'glitches' – faults in the game's code – to create cheats such as running through walls or other impossible moves, so that they can complete the game in the fastest time possible.

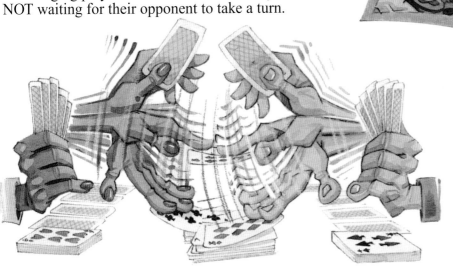

Oh no, strawberry!

TIME FOR A BREAK. Long games can get stressful. In the 1978 World Chess Championship, Viktor Korchnoi wore mirrored sunglasses to hide his eyes from his opponent. He also claimed flavoured yogurts were being used by rival Anatoly Karpov to get coaching from his team.

From idea to game

Do you dream of creating your own game? Board games are usually designed by one or two people, and many early computer games were developed by a small team. But as games become more and more complex, it takes an increasingly wide range of skilled people to build them, from the game designer creating the idea for the game, to modellers and artists creating the graphics, sound designers sculpting the audio, and teams of programmers writing the code that creates the interactions. Then it's the job of testers to play the game over and over on different devices, looking for bugs that need to be fixed.

SPIN-OFF GAMES. Got a great idea? It costs around $100 million or more to make a AAA game, so most releases are games that extend an existing series or concept. Games based on a brand-new idea are much more of a risk because they may not catch on.

THE ART TEAM creates the images, including character designs, props, backgrounds and graphics for controls, known as the UI (user interface). Animators design the characters so that they move in a realistic way.

A GAME DESIGNER comes up with the look and feel of the game, such as the overall concept, storyline and game mechanics (rules). Scriptwriters, level designers and user experience designers work out the details.

SOUND AND MUSIC is an important part of game design, from the right soundtrack for each scene, to sound effects that bring the game world to life or give feedback to the player.

I call this song 'Epic Fail!'

You can do it!

Modern programs like Scratch make it easy to code your own games and animations using sprites (ready-made artwork) and blocks of code you can drag and drop.

DEVELOPERS create the code for the software engines that deliver the game. This requires a mix of technical knowledge, creativity and patience, so that everything works together to create a great experience for the player.

TESTERS play the game over and over to make it crash. They also look for loopholes that will allow players to cheat. Testers are often experienced players who know how to push games and hardware to their limits.

@*Č()$*@!!!

Ah! So that's how you read code . . .

PROJECT MANAGERS are the unsung heroes who keep everything on track. There are often thousands of graphics and sounds in a game, and it's their job to make sure nothing is forgotten.

Is gaming bad for you?

How often has your mum or dad said 'Time's up! Turn that thing off and do something else!' Irritating as it sounds, this is actually good advice. Too much of anything is never good for you, and it's hard to get enough exercise if you're always watching a screen. It is true that certain video games can improve your coordination, while your ability to work out the trickiest levels gives you hope about solving even the most difficult problems. But too much gaming can lead to health issues. Always remember that the best games are the right ones for your age.

For

No, you don't get points for knocking things down!

SPEEDY REFLEXES. The complexity of video games can help gamers develop a better sense of their surroundings, allowing them to drive safely, navigate around town or spot friends in a crowd.

EAGLE EYES. Games can improve your visual skills. One US insurance company found that video games helped older drivers improve the skills they need to drive safely.

SHARP SKILLS. A study of young surgeons found that those who were avid gamers as teenagers tended to have better surgical skills and hand-eye coordination.

Against

HOOKED. One in ten gamers gets hooked on games and finds it incredibly hard to stop, especially when playing online games that have no end.

Top tip

Five signs you're gaming too much:

- When you stop playing, you get upset or bored.
- You spend more time gaming than hanging out with friends.
- It's hard to concentrate at school.
- You lie about how often and long you're gaming.
- You feel guilty about this, but you can't stop.

OVERWEIGHT. Every hour teenagers spend online increases their chances of becoming overweight. However, games where players stand up and mimic sports or dance actions with a controller are a good way of keeping fit.

Hmm… I think you need to widen your interests!

SORE THUMBS. Tapping over and over on a controller can damage tendons and nerves in your thumbs. Slouching is also bad for growing children and teenagers, especially if they play games sitting on the floor or on the bed.

Immersive gaming

The last 30 years have seen a revolution in gaming technology. For many, the future is immersive gaming: the merging of real life and the virtual world. While augmented reality, or AR, mixes the digital world with the real world, in virtual reality (VR), everything you see is generated by a computer. The possibilities are endless: VR and AR are already being used by doctors and teachers, and even to help people overcome their fear of heights or spiders. And remarkably, after spending a few minutes in a VR space, people can recognise each other by the way they move!

VR WITH FRIENDS. In arcades, gamers wearing VR headsets run around an empty warehouse exploring enchanted forests, surfing virtual waves or battling aliens.

Quick...
follow me!

VIRTUAL DOCTORS. AR can help surgeons see inside a patient's body in 3-D, or help nurses find the veins in an arm. In the Netherlands, AR is also being used to send the location of the nearest emergency medical equipment to your phone.

How it works

When you put on a VR headset, your eyes and ears are cut off from reality, tricking your mind into thinking you're somewhere else.

IMMERSIVE LEARNING. VR and AR bring the real world into the classroom. Using AR, students can look inside an exploding volcano or meet a giant dinosaur. With VR, they can visit the interior of an Egyptian pyramid.

WINDOW ON THE WORLD. VR has the power to take people to new places in a completely immersive and revolutionary way. For example, you can swim with dolphins without getting wet!

FUTURE PLANS. Construction and factory workers are already able to see virtual blueprints as they walk around a site, and in the future NASA astronauts will be able to view important schematics laid on top of critical mission systems.

What's the future of gaming?

In the future, robots that can think for themselves, known as artificial intelligence (AI), will open a world of creative possibilities. AI can create robots that are able to develop their own personalities as opposed to just following a script. It will also produce games matched exactly to your skill levels, or create humanlike 'chatbots' you can talk to and play with. But the games we play are always likely to include the same ingredients that delighted our ancient ancestors: skill, luck, strategy and the thrill of competition.

MACHINE LEARNING. In 2016, the Google AlphaGo program defeated the best Go player in the world. It did this by analysing millions of previous human champions and then developing moves that no humans had considered.

In 2006, a brain wave reader known as an electrocorticographic (ECoG) enabled a teenager to play Space Invaders using just his mind to steer left and right. In the future, perhaps all video games will be controlled using just brain power.

UNSTOPPABLE BOTS. In 2017, an OpenAI bot learned from scratch how to play a popular strategy game. After just two weeks, it defeated the best human players in the world by learning how to predict their moves.

ANGRY DROIDS. When human players get pushed into a corner, they get aggressive. And when an AI network competed in a fruit-picking game against other bots, it did exactly the same thing. The more intelligent the network is, the quicker it is to get angry!

GAMIFICATION is turning everyday tasks, like brushing your teeth, into a game by adding points, levels and rewards. The aim – to make real life more challenging. Great job, you've just earned 50 points for reading this sentence!

SERIOUS GAMES are designed to help practise real-life skills, from training firefighter crews and medical teams to planning a supply drop to famine victims.

Glossary

AAA games (pronounced 'triple A') Top-quality games, usually with a huge budget.

Arcade An indoor venue where players pay to play video games, pinball machines, air hockey and other games.

Artificial intelligence (AI) Computers and robots that can simulate human thinking or intelligent behaviour.

Augmented reality A game or program that adds a digital layer to the real world.

Automaton A mechanical device that moves like a human being.

Avatar An icon or character representing a player in a game.

Bitmap An image stored as a series of tiny dots called pixels.

Chatbot A computer program that can mimic a human conversation, using either audio – through a speaker – or text messages. Chatbots are often used to assist customers shopping online.

Cheat Use an alternative playing style or trick to make a game easier.

Clan A group of players who regularly play together in multiplayer games.

Console game A computer game played on a machine that has been specifically designed for playing video games.

Epic win An amazing outcome, usually after a long struggle.

Glitch A minor fault or bug in a game.

Grandmaster A chess expert who wins international competitions.

Graphic A picture or image on a computer screen.

Immersive Software with a 3-D image that surrounds the viewer.

Interaction When a player presses a game control such as a button on a screen.

Joystick A controller consisting of a base and a stick that can be moved in several directions, often by using only one hand.

Mech Room or space packed with gaming equipment.

MMORPG (massively multiplayer online role-playing game) An online game that can support thousands or even millions of players.

Mobile-device games Games that are played on mobile devices such as smartphones and tablets.

Modding Modifying or adding new content to a game.

Ping-pong Another name for table tennis.

Pixel A tiny dot, the basic unit of colour on a computer screen.

Programmer A person who writes computer programs.

Speedrun Using glitches and tricks to play through a game as fast as possible.

Spin-off game A video game that is a close copy of an existing game. Spin-off games are often part of a series.

Sprite A computer graphic that can be moved on a computer screen.

Tangram A Chinese puzzle made up of a square that has been cut into seven pieces. The pieces can be rearranged to create various patterns and shapes, including animals.

Tween Short for tweenager – a child in their early teenage years.

User interface (UI) The controls for a computer or game. Can be a keyboard or a button on a screen.

Vector image Computer-generated image made up of lines or curves.

Virtual reality Game or program where everything you see is created by a computer.

Index

Top game stats

Expert chess players can memorise an incredible 300,000 patterns.

Playing with a 52-card deck, there are 400 billion card combinations, more than the number of stars in the Milky Way.

In 2017, the record for the longest board game marathon was 80 hours, played by four childhood friends from the Netherlands.

In 2014, an English father and son beat the world record for longest ping-pong rally. They played over 16,000 shots in a rally that lasted for 8 hours and 40 minutes – without any bathroom breaks!

The largest game of hide-and-seek was played on New Year's Day in 2014, by 1,437 people in Chengdu, China.

The world's first video game was a simple tennis game invented by US physicist William Higinbotham, working in Brookhaven National Laboratory in 1958.

In 2017, the world spent over $100 billion on games, with over $45 billion of this spent on mobile-device games.

In 2010, the US Air Force built a supercomputer known as Condor Cluster by stringing together 1,760 consoles, making it one of the fastest computers in the world at the time.

The largest arcade machine in the world is taller than an elephant and nearly 2 metres (6 feet) wide. Players have to use a stepladder to play on it!

Games from around the world

Chess was first played in India. The original pieces were shaped like foot soldiers, cavalry, elephants and chariots.

The first known dice were found in an ancient site in Iran known as the Burnt City.

Playing cards were invented in China, along with go, dominoes and mah-jong.

Ping-pong was a party game invented in England in the 1880s.

Senet was first played in ancient Egypt. Players moved their pieces on a board of 30 squares after throwing sticks or bones.

There are more than 200 versions of mancala found in Africa, all played by moving small stones, beans or shells from one 'pit' or 'house' to the next.

The thousands of anime characters found in role-playing, puzzle and digital pet games were created in Japan.

The Checkered Game of Life, Battleship and many other board games were invented by US toy companies. Most early computer games were also invented in US research laboratories.

Did you know?

There are 52 cards in a deck, the same as the number of weeks in a year. And if you add up all the symbols in a deck of cards, there are 365, the number of days in a year.

Italian inventor Leonardo da Vinci designed an automaton in 1495 that looked like an armoured knight – the original fighting robot.

In World War II, the Allies smuggled maps, compasses and banknotes to prisoners of war inside cards and board games.

The name of the game mah-jong means 'sparrows'. The name comes from the sound the tiles make when they are being mixed up. They sound like squabbling birds.

If you laid all the Scrabble tiles ever produced end to end, they would reach around the Earth eight times.

Toru Iwatani created the shape of the Pac-Man character after being inspired by a half-eaten pizza. It was named the most recognisable video game character of all time.

The mushrooms designed by Shigeru Miyamoto for his platform games are based on a real red-and-white mushroom. Beware, eating one in real life will make you horribly sick!